POSITIVE thinking... PURPOSEFUL living

Keeping a Positive Perspective
For a Powerful Change
In Your Daily Life

Inspired by Faith

I0809268

Positive thinking...Purposeful living

ISBN 978-0-9886719-1-1

Published by Product Concept Mfg., Inc.

2175 N. Academy Circle #200, Colorado Springs, CO 80909

Written and Compiled by Vicki J. Kuyper
in association with Product Concept Mfg., Inc.

All scripture quotations are from the King James version of the Bible unless otherwise noted.

Sayings not having a credit listed are contributed by writers for Product Concept Mfg., Inc. or in a rare case, the author is unknown.

POSITIVE thinking... PURPOSEFUL living

Live each day as if your life had just begun.

Johann Wolfgang Von Goethe

If you're the kind of woman who has a glass half-full outlook on life, it doesn't mean your glass is filled with more good things than the glass half-empty folks. It simply means you choose to focus on what you have, how far you've come and the positive possibilities each new day holds. May this little book be a welcome companion that offers you encouragement along the way!

One Thousand Minutes

This is the day which the LORD hath made;
we will rejoice and be glad in it.
Psalm 118:24

Today is a once-in-a-lifetime gift. You never know what you'll see, what you'll do, who you'll meet or what new opportunity will land in your lap. In a mere twenty-four hours, today will become just a memory. If you set aside eight hours for the rest your body needs, you're left with just under 1,000 precious minutes.

You only have one chance to grab hold of the treasures hidden in those fast-moving minutes. Don't let familiarity with your daily routine lull you into missing the beauty and mystery each new day holds. Raise your expectations. God's fingerprints are all around you. Today, be on the lookout for reasons to rejoice. Grab hold of each minute with open arms.

We're All Kids at Heart

As a mother comforts her child,
so will I comfort you.
Isaiah 66:13 NIV

Sometimes, it feels good to be a kid. You're not responsible for all that grown-up stuff like bills, deadlines and putting a healthy meal on the table. That's your parents' job. As a kid, when you're hungry or sad or worried or in pain you turn to them—your mom or dad—with the hope that their kiss will help make it all better.

As a grown woman, it can feel as though the weight of the world is resting on your shoulders. But the truth is, God's in charge, not you. There's only so much you can do. So, do what you can. Then, let go. Let God handle the rest. Find relief in remembering you're His child. Allow Him to be the parent you need right now.

APPLE HARVEST

A word fitly spoken
is like apples of gold in pictures of silver.
Proverbs 25:11

A compliment or word of encouragement is a thing of beauty. Why not keep them where they can continue to lift your spirits when you need it most? If someone sends kind words via email, print them out and place them in a special place along with thank you notes and greeting cards. If you're encouraged by what someone says in conversation, jot down their words in a journal or begin a "blessings" book where you keep track of the blessings you see—and hear—each day.

Then, when you're in need of a "good word" go back and read those you've received in the past. All too often, it's the negative words we repeat over and over in our minds. Refuse to give them any more airtime. Reach for the positive instead.

LOL... IT'S GOOD FOR YOU!

A merry heart
doeth good like a medicine.
Proverbs 17:22

Learning to look on the bright side of life is more than just a sweet sentiment. It's also a healthy habit. Did you know that our bodies consider laughter a form of exercise? When we laugh, our blood pressure and heart rate rise briefly and then drop, just like they do after a workout at the gym. Laughter also increases white blood cells, which in turn fight disease.

So, give yourself a daily dose of a great-tasting medicine. Watch a funny film. Listen to a comedian. Hang out with a friend who tickles your funny bone. Look for the humor in a tense situation. Learn to laugh more easily at yourself. Every giggle and grin you share today can help lead you to a happier, healthier tomorrow.

MATTERS OF THE HEART

Man looketh on the outward appearance,
but the LORD looketh on the heart.
1 Samuel 16:7

As women, it's common to feel under pressure to look a certain way. It seems as though our worth is being measured by the number on a scale, the label on our jeans or the age on our driver's license. But not one of these things says anything about who we really are or what our heart is really like.

God knows, and loves, the true you. He doesn't care where you shop, if your hair needs a trim or if your underarms jiggle when you wave. He accepts you as you are, right here, right now, inside and out. There's nothing you can do, or wear, to make Him love you more...or less. He knows your heart and longs for you to know His.

ALWAYS NEAR

If I take the wings of the morning,
and dwell in the uttermost parts of the sea;
Even there shall thy hand lead me,
and thy right hand shall hold me.
Psalm 139:9–10

Sometimes, life leads us far from the ones we love. A cross-country move or extended business trip can leave us feeling lost in the crowd. At other times, we struggle with emotional distance. We may feel alone in our very own home. But regardless of how isolated we feel, there's Someone who never leaves our side.

God is near, regardless of where you are or what your emotions lead you to believe is true. He's so close, He can hold you in His hand. When your heart is feeling more empty than full, picture your heavenly Father cradling you next to His heart. Tell Him how you feel. He's close enough to hear you whisper.

RECIPE FOR ABUNDANCE

Give, and it will be given to you. A good measure, pressed down, shaken together and running over, will be poured into your lap. For with the measure you use, it will be measured to you.

Luke 6:38 NIV

Exact measurements matter when you're baking. To bake a cake, you carefully measure the flour, tamping it down into the measuring cup and leveling it off with a knife. Too little or too much of one ingredient and your dessert could end in disaster.

Unlike flour, love can't be accurately measured or evenly distributed. It's meant to be showered liberally on those around you, with no thought of return. As you freely love others, something wonderful happens. Love overflows back into your own life. It may not be in the way, or from the person, that you expect. But love flows from a Source that never runs dry. Prepare to be drenched.

SIDE-BY-SIDE

Rejoice with them that do rejoice,
and weep with them that weep.
Romans 12:15

Life has its ups and downs. When those you love are on a downward slope, how can you make a positive difference in their lives? Weep with them. That may sound rather counterintuitive. After all, you want to cheer them up not bring them down even further. But don't be deceived into thinking that if you put on a happy face and dance around their difficulties that they'll forget what's weighing heavy on their hearts.

Instead, ask how they're doing...really. Then, listen. Allow your heart to break right along with theirs. After they feel heard—and are reminded they're not alone in their struggle—they'll be much more receptive to move on to lighter conversation. And when things begin to look up, remember to share in their celebration as wholeheartedly as you have their struggle.

THE GROWING SEASON

He has made every thing beautiful in its time.
He has also set eternity in the human heart.
Ecclesiastes 3:11 NIV

"Now" is a buzzword for modern times. We want our texts to be answered immediately, our coffee to be waiting for us at the drive-thru and those five pounds we gained over Christmas to disappear if we jog once around the block. Previously considered a virtue, today patience seems to have become obsolete.

But God designed the world to revolve on a more relaxed timetable. It takes nine months before a baby is born. Buds bloom and crops ripen at a leisurely pace. Dusk must fully deepen to dark before dawn can break through. When you find yourself feeling antsy, impatient for something to hurry up and happen, take a deep breath. "Now" isn't always the perfect time. "Later" may yield a greater harvest of blessings.

THE UNKNOWN

Trust in the LORD with all thine heart;
and lean not unto thine own understanding.
In all thy ways acknowledge him,
and he shall direct thy paths.
Proverbs 3:5–6

Today, we have answers at our fingertips. If we have internet access, we feel we have access to anything we could possibly ever need to know. But there are some questions that can't be answered by any search engine, no matter how powerful.

It's possible to keep moving forward without knowing all the answers. We may not fully understand how prayer works or what God's plan really is. But if we trust that the God who loves us knows the answers to these questions, we can lean on Him, instead of our own limited understanding. That allows us to move forward with our heads held high.

SOUND TRACK

By day the LORD directs his love,
at night his song is with me—
a prayer to the God of my life.
Psalm 42:8 NIV

It's been scientifically proven that music affects our moods. So why not use it to put a positive spin on the day ahead? Choose music that makes you want to get up and dance, songs that bring back the happiest of memories and make you want to sing along.

Then go ahead and tackle that unpleasant task on your To-Do list, the workout you've been putting off, the bathroom you've dreaded scrubbing or the project you've procrastinated over way too long. Refuse to live today in a minor key. Literally changing the channel to the soundtrack of your life can help you stay in step with where you really want to be.

BEYOND BOUNDARIES

The LORD shall be thy confidence.
Proverbs 3:26

You've got amazing skills. You're a unique mix of talent, knowledge, experience, passion and personality. That's cause for confidence. But even the most highly skilled—and self-assured—people don't get it right every time. When your true confidence lies in something greater than your own abilities, it's easier to risk pushing yourself beyond your comfort zone. Failure doesn't seem as daunting. And success can look wholly different than what you'd previously imagined.

It's been said that, "God works in mysterious ways." This is not only true of how He works in the world, but how He works through you. Ask Him to give you the courage to risk pushing yourself farther than you've gone before. You can be confident He cares about you maturing into the amazing woman He created you to be.

PUDDLE JUMPING

Lo, the winter is past, the rain is over and gone.
Song of Solomon 2:11

Every storm has a beginning and an end. The same is true with the stormy seasons of our lives. They blow in unexpectedly turning our ordered, predictable lives topsy–turvy with unwelcome gusts of grief, disappointment, confusion or fear. God's promised to be right there with us in the storm. But what do we do until the rain has passed?

It's tempting to spend our time searching the skies for signs that the sun is about to break through. But if we're focused on what's off in the distance, we're likely to miss the blessings and opportunities right at our feet. If we can't stop the rain, it's best to learn how to dance in it. Find joy in small things. Today remains a priceless gift, even when the skies are gray.

THE CHOICE IS YOURS

Walk with the wise and become wise.
Proverbs 13:20 NIV

The people closest to us have the greatest influence on us. That means our circle of friends has a direct effect on our own attitudes and actions. So it makes sense to hang out with people we look up to and respect, friends whose character we'd love to have rub off on our own lives.

Our friends aren't perfect, anymore than we are. But if we're honest with ourselves, we know the difference between friends who build us up and those who tear us down. We also know who will tell us the truth about ourselves in a loving way and those who will simply butter us up with what we want to hear. Do yourself a lifelong favor...choose your friends wisely.

X MARKS THE SPOT

Where your treasure is, there will your heart be also.
Matthew 6:21

What do you treasure in life? Really? If you're honest with yourself, it's usually what you spend the most time thinking about, caring for and/or talking about. It's something that if lost or inaccessible would cause you great distress.

What you treasure matters, because what you care about directs the decisions you make. If you treasure fame, you'll put everything else on the sidelines to achieve it. If you treasure fortune, you may cut corners to acquire it. If you treasure people, you'll pour your life into theirs at every opportunity. Only when we treasure what is valuable in God's eyes will we find ourselves holding riches that can't be lost, stolen or decline in value.

RISE AND SHINE

My voice shalt thou hear in the morning, O LORD; in the morning will I direct my prayer unto thee, and will look up.
Psalm 5:3

What's your morning ritual? Take a shower. Grab a cup of coffee. Throw on some mascara so you at least look awake... However you prepare for the day ahead, there's one thing you can do that will help set the tone for the entire day: pray.

By taking just a moment or two to acknowledge God's presence and ask Him to guide you in making wise, loving decisions, you help shift the focus of a me–centered day to a God–centered one. Once you get in the habit of sharing a few words with God, you'll find you have a lot more to talk about. Luckily He hears you just as clearly in the shower or during your morning commute as He does when you're on your knees.

YOU'RE GOLDEN

Do to others what you would have them do to you.
Matthew 7:12 NIV

Little kids are reminded of the Golden Rule over and over again. As adults, perhaps we could use a bit of a refresher course. What kindness, word of encouragement or help could you use today? Ask God to help you notice someone else who shares a similar need. Then, give what you'd love to receive. Literally.

The more aware we are of the needs of others, the less our own problems seem to overwhelm us. It's a win-win situation! As we practice loving others well, a little bit of that love rubs right back onto us. Treating others the way we'd love to be treated not only makes good sense, it yields great rewards to everyone involved.

A "GOOD" CRY

God shall wipe away all tears from their eyes.
Revelation 7:17

God promises there will be a time when weeping is a thing of the past. Until then, tears are going to happen. But when you feel the urge to let the tears fall, consider this bit of advice: People are worth your tears. Things...not so much.

There are big things in life...and small ones. If we get in the habit of treating little disappointments and inconveniences as though they are a matter of life and death, we begin to lose perspective on what's actually significant. This doesn't mean we should make light of the pain in our lives. But we need to give it only as much weight, and as many tears, as it truly deserves.

THE CRAZY QUILT OF LIFE

We know that all things work together for good to them that love God.
Romans 8:28

Is today a "good" day or a "bad" day? What has led you to label it that way? With God, even what we consider a bad day can be transformed into something good. That's because God takes the tatters of our heartaches and broken dreams and weaves them together into something totally new.

In the same way that a gifted quilter can transform scraps of an out-dated (and at times, absolutely hideous) outfit into something that's not only warm and useful, but surprisingly beautiful, God repurposes the experiences we'd rather forget in innovative ways. They may teach us, lead us in an unexpected direction, help us connect with a new friend... With God's help, we can trust that even our worst days hold the promise of something good.

WISE WORDS

Where no counsel is, the people fall:
but in the multitude of counsellors there is safety.
Proverbs 11:14

A popular proverb states, "It takes a village to raise a child." Even if childhood is just a distant memory, we still need a "village" in our lives. We need people around us who really know us, who want the best for us and who are willing to walk alongside us when life gets hard. These are more than "fair weather" friends. These are people who not only won't give up on us when we blow it—but continue to encourage us not to give up on ourselves.

When you're facing difficulties or a major decision, pray about it. But don't stop there. Call on your "village" for advice. They can help you see your situation, and a positive resolution, from a whole new perspective.

A QUIET SPOT

Be still, and know that I am God.
Psalm 46:10

Stop...for just a moment. Turn off the TV or music. Power down your phone. Find a quiet spot where you can sit without distraction. Close your eyes and say, "Hello, God. It's me." Then, simply sit in God's presence and listen.

Some people find it harder to turn off their brain than to disconnect from their electronic devices. But taking time to quiet our thoughts is one way we become more aware of God's still, small voice speaking into our lives. We are so rarely quiet—inside or out. But the more comfortable we are with silence, the more we become conscious of the fact that we are not alone. God is near—and He's more involved in this life than we ever imagined.

THE HALF-EMPTY BLUES

*Can any one of you by worrying
add a single hour to your life?*
Matthew 6:27 NIV

Worry can turn a half-full attitude upside-down, draining optimism and hope right out of your life. The good news is you have a built-in warning system. Worry can't creep in unannounced. It's heralded by a noisy entourage of negative voices. If you let them mumble on without shutting them down, you grow accustomed to their critical, pessimistic words. Soon, you're feeling helpless and depressed.

So, when those negative thoughts start murmuring, silence them. Refuse to play "what if..." Focus on what's true, what's good and what you can do, instead of what you can't. The only thing worry can do is make you feel bad. It has no power to change anything. Picture yourself placing every worry in God's capable hands—and refuse to snatch them back.

ON SOLID GROUND

The Sovereign LORD is my strength;
he makes my feet like the feet of a deer,
he enables me to tread on the heights.
Habakkuk 3:19 NIV

As we age, there's a lot of hype about how important it is to strengthen our core. After all, we don't want to get wobbly, trip and break a hip! But while there is positive value in adding weight-bearing exercise to our schedule to help us remain balanced, stable and strong, there's also value in strengthening our spiritual core.

The more we invite God into the small things in our lives, instead of just calling on Him when everything is falling to pieces, the more stable and sure-footed we'll feel in our everyday lives. He's our true core, the "rock of ages" that will never give way beneath our feet.

LET'S REVIEW...

Thus saith the LORD of hosts;
Consider your ways.
Haggai 1:7

When life is moving along fairly smoothly, it's tempting to just keep plowing ahead with minimal introspection. But there's always room for improvement, within our lives and within ourselves. Instead of sliding into an "if it ain't broke, don't fix it" attitude, why not treat every day as a welcome opportunity for growth?

Before you fall asleep, take a moment to review... and consider. What did I do that made a positive difference? Is there anywhere I fell short? Are there any words I wish I could take back? Is there anything I need to make right? Are there any lessons I can learn from today that will help me forge a better tomorrow? A well-examined life has the best chance of becoming a life well-lived.

AN ATTITUDE OF GRATITUDE

Give thanks in all circumstances;
for this is God's will for you.
1 Thessalonians 5:18 NIV

Need a face lift? Count your blessings. That's sure to bring a boost of joy to your heart and a smile to your face. Even on our toughest days, we have reason to be grateful. When we take a moment to bring to mind what we have to be thankful for, instead of feeling burdened or bitter we begin to feel blessed. And so we are.

Get in the habit of making every day Thanksgiving. Thank God for five things you're especially grateful for. It could be friends and family, food in your pantry, a car that runs, a beautiful sunrise or a job that helps pay the bills. You'll find that listing five blessings jumpstarts your mind to come up with more. That's how an attitude of gratitude gets its start.

HOPE REALLY DOES FLOAT

Now the God of hope fill you
with all joy and peace in believing,
that ye may abound in hope.
Romans 15:13

A positive attitude is buoyed by hope. That's because hope acts as a kind of life preserver for your heart. When your heart is heavy and starts to weigh your optimism down, hope provides the assurance you need to help hold your head up through the storm.

Hope is not a "close your eyes and blow out your birthday candles" kind of wish that things will turn out for the best. It's the assurance that God is at work behind the scenes. He sees you. He knows you. He loves you. And He's promised He has great things in store for you.

WITH EWE IN MIND

The LORD is my shepherd; I shall not want.
He maketh me to lie down in green pastures:
he leadeth me beside the still waters.
He restoreth my soul.
Psalm 23:1–3

Sheep are not known for their high IQ. You can't train them to fetch your slippers or the morning paper. The only thing they're really good at is following the crowd. They flock together and follow whomever happens to be out in front. That's why a shepherd comes in handy. He's wise enough to lead the sheep to where they need to go.

It isn't very flattering, but sometimes we're likely to have sheep–like tendencies. We mindlessly go along with the crowd. But if we seek God's guidance, He'll help us more easily recognize when we need to break away from the flock and blaze a fresh path.

GOING AGAINST THE GRAIN

Iron sharpeneth iron;
so a man sharpeneth the countenance of his friend.
Proverbs 27:17

Any criticism is hard to hear. Often, our initial reaction is to defend ourselves, to make excuses (even if we don't say them aloud) as to why this assessment is inaccurate, unkind or unfair. But if we stop and listen before we immediately discount what we hear, we may discover we're recipients of a valuable gift we not only can use, but really need.

Consider every critique a piece of sandpaper. If that sandpaper is held by someone you know and respect, allow it to do its work. (We all have rough edges that could use a bit of smoothing!) Ask God for wisdom in sorting truth from opinion. Then do the unthinkable. Thank the person for their words and take any truth they've shared to heart.

TRASH PICK UP

As far as the east is from the west,
so far hath he removed our transgressions from us.
Psalm 103:12

Imagine lugging a trash bag, bulging with refuse, around with you wherever you go. Not only does it never leave your side, on occasion you paw through its contents, scrutinizing every piece of rubbish, then carefully placing it back inside.

Sounds ridiculous, right? But every time we refuse to let go of something we've done wrong, we're choosing to haul garbage around with us. Whether it's an honest mistake or an outright bad choice, anything we regret having done is done. We can't change the past. We can only change what we do with it. Apologize. Make amends. Then take God at His word. If we ask Him for forgiveness, we have it. Learn from the past, then leave it behind.

BEAUTY TREATMENT

I will praise thee;
for I am fearfully and wonderfully made:
marvellous are thy works;
and that my soul knoweth right well.
Psalm 139:14

There are miraculous natural wonders in this world...the majesty of the redwoods, the glory of the Grand Canyon, the enormity of the blue whale, the delicacy of a dandelion's seeds and intricacy of each individual flake of snow. Yet above all of the marvelous creations of this universe and beyond, our Creator has declared us—people—His incomparable masterpiece.

Yet we so rarely view ourselves this way. We nit pick over perceived flaws, viewing ourselves and others with a critical, comparative eye. Want to see things in a more positive, accurate light? Try looking at yourself (and others) through God's eyes. That's a mirror that never lies.

UNSHAKEABLE

I am the LORD, I change not.
Malachi 3:6

It's often said that nothing stays the same. That's not entirely true. There is one thing that always was, always is and always will be without change. That's God's character. His love, grace, goodness and generosity never waver. He isn't swayed by emotion, hormones or peer pressure. He's never fickle or flighty. When God makes a promise, He follows through. Without fail.

What a great encouragement to know that we can trust the One who holds our very breath in His hands to remain constant in His love and care. Our circumstances will change. Other relationships will change. Our bodies will change. But regardless of the whirlwind that may be taking place in other areas of our lives, God remains faithful—our calm, unchanging eye of the storm.

DON'T LOOK AWAY

Whoever is kind to the poor lends to the LORD,
and he will reward them for what they have done.
Proverbs 19:17 NIV

They're on the street corner holding a sign: "Please help." They're standing in line at the soup kitchen. They're hustling for change in the subway. They're somewhere around the world where you'll never travel, slowly starving to death. They may be living right next-door.

Everywhere we look, there are people in need. We rationalize, "We can't help them all..." But we can make a difference to someone. Today. Don't look away. If you feel the nudge to give, give. Give whether you have plenty or just enough. If you can't give anything else, give a smile. One day you may find yourself on the receiving end.

FLYING HIGH

They that wait upon the LORD shall renew their strength;
they shall mount up with wings as eagles;
they shall run, and not be weary;
and they shall walk, and not faint.
Isaiah 40:31

Life is just so, well...daily. There is no pause or rewind button when you need a break. There are only so many vacation days, and vacations not only cost money, but often wind up being more stressful than whatever it is we happen to be vacating from.

So the next time you find yourself tired, discouraged or simply lacking a sense of anticipation and purpose in your life, take a God break. Ask God for the strength you need to persevere through whatever you need to do. Picture Him with His arm around your shoulder, helping you continue moving forward, step-by-step. He's a companion who'll never tire, a life coach who always knows what we need to hear.

SEEING THE UNSEEN

I meditate on all thy works;
I muse on the work of thy hands.
Psalm 143:5

It can be hard to catch a glimpse of an invisible God. Our relationship with Him is unlike any other. We can't see Him, speak to Him, hug Him or connect with Him in the same way we do with anyone else in our lives. Maybe that's why it's so easy to forget He's there.

That's why it's helpful to have something to jog our memory. Keep a stack of 3 x 5 cards near your bed. Before you lay down each night, jot down ways you've experienced God's hand at work in the world. It could be through a Bible verse, an answer to prayer, the actions of a friend or beauty of His creation. Anytime God's presence feels distant, read what you've written...and remember.

A JOYOUS PERSPECTIVE

Though the fig tree does not bud
and there are no grapes on the vines,
though the olive crop fails and the fields produce no food...
yet I will rejoice in the LORD, I will be joyful in God my Savior.
Habakkuk 3:17–18 NIV

Joy flows naturally when things are going our way. When our marriage is strong, the cancer is in remission, the list of layoffs does not include our name—when our current life story feels worthy of Christmas newsletter status.

But what about the other times? That's when supernatural joy takes over. The closer we draw to God, the more we begin to see things through His eyes. Only God can take a positive "glass half-full" perspective and transform it into a "glass overflowing like an artesian well" outlook on life. If you're searching for joy, go straight to the Source.

CONTROLLED BURN

He that is slow to anger is better than the mighty; and he that ruleth his spirit than he that taketh a city.
Proverbs 16:32

Anger has its place. When we witness injustice, cruelty or a selfish disregard for others, anger is a reasonable (and at times even righteous) reaction. But anger often springs from a much less noble source. Our feelings get hurt. Our orders aren't obeyed. Our plans are disrupted. At times like these, it's easy to react first and think later.

However, if we allow our anger to control us, we're likely to say or do something we'll later regret. Furthermore, a lack of self-control instantly whittles a positive attitude down to a negative one. So, when anger starts to sizzle: stop, breathe and pray. Ask God for wisdom, honesty and humility. Rule your anger. Don't allow it to rule you.

WHO DO YOU LOOK UP TO?

Who can find a virtuous woman?
for her price is far above rubies.
Proverbs 31:10

If those who knew you best were to describe your character, would the word "virtuous" come up? How about descriptions such as "admirable," "good," or "worthy of respect"? A virtuous woman is honest and above reproach. She's what would be described in days gone by as a "decent" woman.

In our current culture, "virtuous" isn't considered much of a compliment. Sexy, shrewd and successful...that's what we really admire. How about you? What traits do you hold in high esteem? Ultimately, those traits are the ones you'll strive to attain in your own life. Choose carefully what's worthy of your admiration.

PEACE TIME

Peace I leave with you, my peace I give unto you:
not as the world giveth, give I unto you.
Let not your heart be troubled, neither let it be afraid.
John 14:27

It's impossible to find peace in a world with 24-hour news coverage. That's why peace has got to be an inside job. The kind of peace God promises is not an escape from heartache, tears or even questions that begin with "why?" It runs deeper than that.

The peace of God is more like a sense of trust that allows you to continue on in spite of the tragedy and evil that is present in this world. It allows you to hold onto hope, even when a situation appears hopeless. It's at the heart of a positive attitude, without bordering on Pollyanna. Draw close to God. Only He can draw you in the direction of true peace.

ONGOING CONSTRUCTION SITE

Encourage one another and build each other up,
just as in fact you are doing.
1 Thessalonians 5:11 NIV

Our words have power. We can use them to build someone up or tear someone down. But if we want to nurture a positive outlook on life, there's really only one choice: Follow in the footsteps of our favorite superhero and use our power for good, not evil!

A kind word cost nothing more than a few seconds of our time. As we can attest from personal experience anytime we've been on the receiving end of a compliment, that time is well spent. The more we get in the habit of looking for the good in life, the more we'll notice those involved in making good things happen. We don't have to be effusive with our praise, just sincere. Build something beautiful today by sharing an encouraging word.

FAITH AND YOUR 40%

Happy is that people, whose God is the LORD.
Psalm 144:15

Research tells us that 50% of our "happiness quotient" is determined by genetics. How happy we feel is influenced by the temperament we're born with. Another 10% is swayed by circumstances—the things we can't control in our lives. But that final 40% that determines how happy we are is totally up to us. We choose what we're going to do with our time, our talents, our relationships and our circumstances.

Turning to God with the details of our daily life can play a positive part in that 40%. The comfort, peace, joy and love we receive from our relationship with God can help us find our "happy place" right here, right now.

SLEEP IN HEAVENLY PEACE

Thy sleep shall be sweet.
Proverbs 3:24

God was so wise in creating us so that we need to come to a complete stop at the end of the day. We need to turn off our brains, relax our bodies and drift into a place where dreaming is the only item on our agenda. Being tired is a gift that's heaven-sent. It's God's gentle nudge, reminding us that we've done all we can today. It's time to put today to bed (literally) in preparation for a productive tomorrow.

There will be nights when sleep doesn't come as easily as we'd like. Consider those nights "gifts," as well. Instead of tossing and turning, try talking to God about what's running through your mind. Tell Him everything. He won't be offended if you nod off in mid-conversation.

DREAM THE IMPOSSIBLE DREAM

I can do all things through Christ
which strengtheneth me.
Philippians 4:13

How do you view yourself? Strong? Capable? Confident? Your self-image is more than who you are in your mind. It makes a difference in how you live out your life. If you view yourself as a victim, you'll act like one. But if you believe what God says is true—that He will give you the strength to handle everything that He sets before you—you can no longer play the victim. You become who you were created to be, the heroine of your own story.

It's God who enables you to live up to this role. He doesn't promise it'll be easy or that you'll never fail along the way. But as you rely on Him for strength, you'll find yourself doing things you would have never dreamed possible on your own.

PASSING IT ON

Praise be to...the God of all comfort,
who comforts us in all our troubles,
so that we can comfort those in any trouble
with the comfort we ourselves receive from God.
2 Corinthians 1:3–4 NIV

Comfort is a good thing. We look for it in shoes, in recliners and even in food. We also look for it in people. What's amazing is that the more uncomfortable we are in life, the more of a comfort we may become to others.

When we face stressful, painful situations, God helps us find the comfort we need to console and cheer us. Through our own experience, we become more adept at comforting and consoling others. We have a better understanding of what it's like to walk a mile in their shoes—their very uncomfortable shoes. As we walk alongside others who are going through difficult times, we can offer reassurance and solace, knowing that one day they'll be given the opportunity to do the same for someone else.

THE GIFT OF TRUTH

An honest answer is like a kiss on the lips.
Proverbs 24:26 NIV

"Do these pants make my hips look big?" There are some questions we may dread answering. But truth is always preferable to lies, even when the lies are little white ones. At times we may try to convince ourselves that we are simply being "economical with the truth," shielding someone's feelings beneath a blanket of dishonesty. In the long run, we are doing a disservice to others, as well as to ourselves.

Consider tact truth's Siamese twin. We need to think before we speak, choosing our words as carefully as we do the perfect gift. An honest answer should be as gentle as a kiss, bestowed with love and tenderness at the appropriate time and place.

YOU CAN COUNT ON ME

He that is faithful in that which is least
is faithful also in much.
Luke 16:10

In general, people are pretty consistent. How we do little things is how we end up doing big things. If we're careful counting our pennies throughout the year, we'll be careful with how we spend our Christmas bonus. If we put forth our very best efforts in a temporary work position, chances are we'll do the same with a more permanent one.

When it comes to spiritual things, the same holds true. If we share the little details of our day with God, we'll certainly want to include Him in the ones that rock our world. The more faithful we are in relying on God, the more He can rely on us to spread His love to those around us, in both big and little ways.

EMPLOY A POSITIVE OUTLOOK

Every man should eat and drink,
and enjoy the good of all his labour, it is the gift of God.
Ecclesiastes 3:13

There's a difference between looking forward to the weekend—and living for it. It's great to have some down time, to kick back and enjoy some fun. But there's much more to life than Friday nights, vacation days and retirement.

We spend the majority of our lives eating, sleeping and working. Whether the work we do is at home, at school or at a place of employment, there are good things to be found there. There are challenges to be faced, skills to be honed and accomplishments to be achieved. Focus on doing the best you can with what you have right where you are. Whether you're at work or play, there's joy to be found.

HE'S HERE

In him we live, and move, and have our being.
Acts 17:28

"Bidden or not bidden, God is present," is a Latin proverb that psychologist Carl Jung had carved above his front door—and later was carved onto his tombstone. Perhaps it's because this truth is so easy to forget, yet so powerful when remembered.

We may not always be aware of God's presence, but that doesn't make Him any less aware of us or less involved in our lives. From that very first miracle when one of our cells divided into two, God's hand was at work. That deserves more than an occasional "thank you." It deserves our awe, humility, devotion and praise. What can you do today to express to God what His presence means to you?

DO YOURSELF A FAVOR

Do not seek revenge or bear a grudge.
Leviticus 19:18 NIV

Every gift you give to others rubs off a bit on you. If you share good things, you'll feel good. If you hand off a lousy gift, such as one created in anger and delivered as "pay back" for some wrong you feel you've received, you'll feel lousy. Sure, you might enjoy a transitory feeling of vindication, but you've moved farther away from reconciliation. Striking back won't do anything to erase the hurt you feel.

God says that "revenge" is His affair, not ours. People reap the rewards of their own actions in one way or another. So don't let someone else's poor choices lead you to make equally poor choices. Confront what needs to be confronted, if need be. Just do so from a place of restoration, not justification.

TRUE INSIGHT

Where there is no vision, the people perish.
Proverbs 29:18

Helen Keller said, "The only thing worse than being blind is having sight but no vision." There is only so much of this life we can see with our eyes. The rest we have to perceive with our heart, our imagination, our foresight, our discernment and our faith. This kind of vision we label "insight" because with it we're able to fill in the part of the big picture our eyes cannot see.

Do you have a vision for your future? For the kind of woman you want to become in the next five, ten or fifty years? Once you can mentally picture the possibilities, you can take appropriate steps to lead you in the proper direction to help your inner vision become an external reality.

AN ACCURATE MEASURE

Humble yourselves in the sight of the Lord,
and he shall lift you up.
James 4:10

Consider humility a measuring stick. To humble yourself doesn't mean that you slouch down to make yourself seem less than you are. It means you measure up to your true "height." No more, no less. A humble person doesn't put on airs or false modesty in an attempt to appear to be someone she's not. She's the same person in private that she is in public. She's simply herself—and that's enough.

True humility teaches us that we cannot measure ourselves against others, only against ourselves. After all, we're individuals. We're each born with a unique set of standards. We choose whether to live up to whom God created us to be or to make choices that hinder us in fulfilling that potential. Which will you choose today?

GO STRAIGHT TO THE SOURCE

A merry heart maketh a cheerful countenance.
Proverbs 15:13

Where do smiles come from? We can plaster them on, forcing our face to strike a seemingly pleasant pose. But, why? The warmest smiles are spontaneous and homegrown, sprouting from the inside out. They're not only attractive; they're contagious.

The seeds of each smile lie in our own heart. We water them with our very own thoughts. If we focus on the good in life—things that make God Himself smile—our face will reflect our inner outlook. So, focus on what's loveable in others. Be mindful of the blessings you receive each day. Incorporate what you love to do in with what you have to do. Search for ways you can brighten someone else's day. You'll find smiles close at hand...and heart.

SPRING CLEANING

If any man be in Christ, he is a new creature:
old things are passed away;
behold, all things are become new.
2 Corinthians 5:17

When you clean out your closet, you get rid of what no longer fits or is out of style. That ugly Christmas sweater you received as a gift, the sequin jumpsuit you dieted your way into for that disco party...hasta la vista!

God wants to help you do the same thing with your character. Out with the old and in with the new. Anger issues? Prideful? Insecure? Trade them in for patience, humility and confidence. Traits that do not reflect God's own character no longer fit the woman you are today. God's put your past behind you. Leave it there. Working together with God, you'll receive a makeover that brings out the beauty of the new, true you.

GIVING OTHERS A LIFT

Carry each other's burdens.
Galatians 6:2 NIV

How do you get a couch into a second floor apartment? With help! Some things are just too big to carry by ourselves. This is not only true in the physical realm, but also emotionally and spiritually. Life is not a solo act. Yes, God is always there, giving us the strength to carry on. But He's given us something else to help us when we're carrying a heavy load—other people.

We were created to give aid to and receive aid from one another. So, don't wait for others to ask for your help. Offer it as soon as you notice someone in need. A helping hand, a listening ear, an encouraging word, a resource you can share...give what you can when you can.

LET US PRAY

In every thing by prayer and supplication with thanksgiving let your requests be made known unto God. And the peace of God, which passeth all understanding, shall keep your hearts and minds through Christ Jesus.
Philippians 4:6–7

"Prayer changes things" is a popular adage found on everything from pillows to bumper stickers. But is it simply a sweet sentiment or a life-changing reality?

Prayer doesn't always "change" what we expect. Yes, there are times when circumstances and attitudes are transformed in ways we can only attribute to God's mighty hand. But sometimes, what prayer changes lies much closer to home. It changes our hearts and minds with peace, perspective and a better understanding of who God is and how He loves us. It allows us to let go of worry and anxiety. Yes, prayer most certainly changes things. Most of all, it changes the one who prays.

LOVE IN ACTION

A friend loveth at all times.
Proverbs 17:17

Love is more than just a sentiment on a greeting card. It's an action that speaks louder than words. It's something that can be seen and felt without being heard. Love does the right thing, even if it doesn't always appear to be the "nice" thing.

For instance, if a friend asks us to help her stick to her diet, and then invites us to head to a bakery for an emotional binge, the loving thing to do would be to suggest sharing a walk or a cup of tea and conversation instead. The choice is up to her—and we'll love her regardless of her choice. But a true friend always seeks what's in the best interest of those she loves.

POWER SURGE

No one can serve two masters.
Either you will hate the one and love the other,
or you will be devoted to the one and despise the other.
You cannot serve both God and money.
Matthew 6:24 NIV

Everyone serves a "higher power." For some people, that power is God. But there are plenty of other "masters" we willingly give power to in our lives. Things like money, fame, pleasure or the desire to be liked or admired can be cruel taskmasters. They can drain peace, joy, and balance from our lives in countless ways.

Choosing to follow God, to allow His power to work in us and through us, will make a positive change in our lives. God never forces Himself on us. He enters by invitation only. Take a close look at the power source you're plugging into today. Make certain it's one that delivers a positive charge.

INHALE, EXHALE...

Stand still,
and consider the wondrous works of God.
Job 37:14

It's nice we don't have to think about breathing. There are so many other things on our minds... like deadlines, health concerns, relational struggles, finances and that Everest-sized pile of laundry overflowing the hamper. But when your mind starts racing like Seabiscuit around everything that's currently piled on your plate, it's time to override your involuntary respiration and take breathing back into your own hands.

Slow your breathing, inhaling and exhaling as deeply as you can, for just a moment or two. Close your eyes while you're at it. Consider the wondrous gift God's given you by allowing your body to work so efficiently on auto-pilot. Thank Him by exhaling all the way down to your toes. It will not only help clear your head, but calm your heart.

RIDE 'EM, COWGIRL!

Overcome evil with good.
Romans 12:21

In the old black and white Westerns, everyone knew the cowboy in the white hat would win out in the end. In real life, it's harder to tell the good guys from the bad guys. But with every decision you make, you choose which side you'll be on. Go for the white hat.

It's been said that good guys finish last. But that viewpoint doesn't line up with God's. He promises good will overcome evil. That your positive efforts will be rewarded. That your love will make a difference in this world. You may not see the results firsthand. They may not even occur in your lifetime. But the good you do, and the love you share, are guaranteed to be a positive force in an often negative world.

NEVER LET GO

I am persuaded, that neither death, nor life, nor angels, nor principalities, nor powers, nor things present, nor things to come, Nor height, nor depth, nor any other creature, shall be able to separate us from the love of God.

Romans 8:38–39

Think back to what it was like to be a small child clinging to the hand of an adult in unfamiliar surroundings. There was nothing scarier than fearing you'd lose hold of that hand and get lost in the crowd. You need never fear that will happen with your heavenly Father. Nothing can tear you away from His loving care. Not even death.

Even if life leads you through circumstances that cast menacing shadows on every side of you, there's cause for hope, confidence and optimism. God's got your back—and your front and your inside and outside. He's on your side. Period.

GALLERY OPENING

Since the creation of the world God's invisible qualities—
his eternal power and divine nature—
have been clearly seen, being understood
from what has been made, so that people are without excuse.
Romans 1:20 NIV

If you visit a gallery, you can learn about Picasso by studying his art. You can't meet him face-to-face, but you can tell he was an artistic, "out of the box" thinker who wasn't afraid to take risks. You can understand His character through what he's made.

The same can be said for God. Take a look at the "gallery" of His universe. What can you learn about Him? For starters, it's apparent that He's creative, likes diversity and pays attention to the tiniest detail. Evidence of God is all around us. We simply need to explore His gallery with our eyes and our heart open wide.

GREAT EXPECTATIONS

Weeping may endure for a night,
but joy cometh in the morning.
Psalm 30:5

Want to boost your spirits? Bask in a bit of anticipation. What's on your calendar that you're looking forward to? If you can't find something, plan something. It can be as simple as coffee with a friend or as big as a trip across the globe. Thinking about the joy that's headed your way will help make your path a bit smoother where you are right now.

Anticipating what's to come and reminiscing about good times past are both wonderful, momentary diversions. Consider the savory aromas wafting from the kitchen before and after an incredibly memorable meal. They aren't meant to linger forever. After all, you live in the here and now. But they can add a lovely little burst of joy to help brighten an otherwise dreary day.

ACT YOUR AGE

Gray hair is a crown of splendor.
Proverbs 16:31 NIV

The next time you find a gray hair, before you pluck it, thank God for it. It's a sign of life and growth. It's like a button that reads: I'm too old to die young! And that's a privilege, not a curse.

So forgo the black balloons on your next birthday. Regard your wrinkles as you do your favorite jeans, as attire that's comfortably well-worn. Don't lie about your age. Celebrate it! You've been given a priceless gift...time. Only you can choose how to spend the days you've been given. And only by letting go of the younger woman you were can you embrace the mature woman you've become. As for tomorrow, it's a hope, not a guarantee. So delight in the blessings of today—gray hairs and all.

A VERBAL SPARK

A soft answer turneth away wrath.
Proverbs 15:1

Heated words can lead to a relational meltdown. But there's something you can do to turn things around. Refuse to add fuel to the fire. Douse it with cool, reasonable words and a soft verbal tone.

Lowering the volume of a heated interaction will mean those involved will have to tone down their own words to hear what you have to say. That one little adjustment can help the interaction become less emotional and more rational. Sometimes people aren't looking for a conversation. What they want is a fight. If that's the case, simply state (quietly) that you respect their opinion, but will continue the discussion at another time, when passions have cooled and you're both ready to listen, as well as speak.

FIND YOUR OWN PATH

The Lord is my helper,
and I will not fear what man shall do unto me.
Hebrews 13:6

How many of the decisions you make are influenced by what others think and say? What you wear? The car you drive? How you spend your free time? How you raise your children? What you believe about God and yourself? Peer pressure isn't just something that's experienced in High School. It's present in every season of our lives. But how much we allow that influence to shape who we are and what we do is up to us.

Don't let fear—masquerading as a desire for acceptance—carve out the path you'll follow in this life. Have the courage to forge a new path, one that leads you closer to God and to becoming the amazing woman you were created you to be.

WHO DO YOU TURN TO?

I will turn their mourning into joy, and will comfort them, and make them rejoice from their sorrow.
Jeremiah 31:13

We like to be comfortable. That's why things like sweatpants, comfort food, loafers and easy chairs are so popular. There's nothing wrong with feeling at ease. But when your discomfort is emotional, becoming a couch potato or burying your face in an oversized bowl of mac 'n cheese does nothing to cure your condition. You may feel better—or at least distracted—for a while. But soon you'll feel just as miserable as you did before. Sometimes, even worse.

God's a source of comfort that heals us from the inside out. When we trust in Him, instead of things like food, shopping or entertainment to lift our spirits, we'll never feel guilty afterwards. Just blessed.

THE ROYAL TREATMENT

By love, serve one another.
Galatians 5:13

The message is emblazoned on t–shirts and splashed in rhinestones on the backside of jeans: Diva. Princess. Spoiled. It seems that women today are demanding to be pampered, indulged, coddled and served. But will this really help us achieve a happier, more positive approach to life?

When we expect others to cater to our needs, we put ourselves above them. We act as though our time, our comfort and our happiness is more valuable than their own. We also miss out on the opportunity to demonstrate sacrificial love. There's something about giving, instead of always getting, that encourages both our compassion and our gratitude to grow. It helps us keep life, and love, in the proper perspective. That's a royal treatment we can all benefit from.

ACROSS THE MILES

As cold waters to a thirsty soul,
so is good news from a far country.
Proverbs 25:25

Email and the social network have made the world seem smaller. We can take a peek at what's going on in the lives of those we love with a single click. But clicking isn't the same as connecting. Maintaining long-lasting relationships requires communication that goes deeper than a 140-character post.

Today, do something novel. Connect with someone across the miles in an "old-fashioned" way. Call a friend you haven't heard from in awhile, instead of texting. Send a greeting card or hand-written letter via snail mail, instead of cyberspace. Afterward, you may even want to book a trip to reconnect in person. Don't allow time and miles to fade a friendship. There's no treasure more important, or more worthy of keeping in mint condition, than a circle of friends.

GRAB HOLD OF TODAY

Whoso findeth me findeth life.
Proverbs 8:35

It's possible to exist without really living. You can eat and breathe and work and age without being fully aware of the beauty, blessing and opportunity that surrounds you each and every day. But to live—to really live—you need to do more than simply go through the motions. You need to grab hold of what God has placed within your reach.

What new treasure is He extending to you today? A chance to learn and grow? A new relationship—or a greater depth of love and joy with those you already know? An opportunity to explore new sights, new sounds, new tastes, new ways of thinking? An invitation to push yourself beyond yesterday's limits? Ask God to help you see, and risk, acting on a limited time offer by taking advantage of the benefits of today.

HELP TO HEAL

He healeth the broken in heart,
and bindeth up their wounds.
Psalm 147:3

As a kid, an adhesive bandage and a kiss were considered the cure-all for our minor wounds. But as we grow older, we realize that our physical wounds are often less painful (and less stubborn to heal) than our emotional ones. But what Mom told us way back when is still good advice: clean the wound before bandaging it.

When we're in pain emotionally, it's tempting to simply cover it up and try to get on with life. But if we do, our pain often festers, instead of healing. That's why it's so important to bring our broken heart to the One who made it. Show God where it hurts. His wisdom, comfort and love will help cleanse the wound so it can heal properly—and permanently.

RAIN, RAIN...GO AWAY!

A continual dropping in a very rainy day
and a contentious woman are alike.
Proverbs 27:15

There's nothing quite like a persistent drizzle to dampen your spirits. But sometimes the cold front you feel emanates from a person, instead of an actual weather pattern. Even worse, on occasion that person may be you.

A negative, critical attitude can drag down the positive energy in a room as effectively as a black cloud can block the warmth of the sun. Blame it on hormones, a bad hair day or a pessimistic personality. Being touchy and argumentative isn't doing anyone any favors: the contentious person or those in her vicinity. If you're feeling out-of-sorts, don't take it out on those around you—take it to God. Get to the root of the problem and deal with it. Refuse to allow your bad mood to rain on anyone else's parade.

GO FOR THE GREEN

I give every green plant for food.
Genesis 1:30 NIV

Imagine filling your car's fuel tank with black coffee, tossing in an apple danish for good measure and then expecting your automobile to run properly. Chances are you won't make it very far. After all, your car wasn't designed to run on caffeine and sugar. Neither are you.

We have access to an endless array of tempting treats. But our bodies function most efficiently on a balanced diet of lean protein and dairy, whole grains, fruits and veggies. When our bodies work well, we not only feel better physically, but emotionally and mentally. Want to have a more positive outlook on life? Give your body the fuel it needs. Today, why not change out your coffee break for a veggie break?

A POSITIVE INFLUENCE

The LORD, The LORD God, merciful and gracious, longsuffering, and abundant in goodness and truth.
Exodus 34:6

Hanging out with people we trust is bound to have a positive effect on our mood. We don't have to watch our back or try to act like someone we're not. We can relax and simply be ourselves.

God has the kind of character we can trust. That means we can relax when we're in His presence. We don't have to worry about saying the right words when we pray or wearing the right clothes to impress Him. He accepts us exactly as we are. But He doesn't want us to stay there. He's the kind of friend that encourages us to keep on growing, to push our limits and live up to our potential. That's a Friend worth getting to know.

SILENCE CAN BE ELOQUENT

A word spoken in due season,
how good is it!
Proverbs 15:23

It's often said that "Timing is everything." That's certainly true when it comes to saying the right word at the right time. But that doesn't happen by accident. It takes insight and forethought. Sometimes, it takes enough self-control to keep our mouth shut until the proper season rolls around!

Not every thought in our heads needs to be expressed with our mouths. If we get in the habit of giving our full attention to the one who is speaking, instead of using that time to formulate what we want to say next, we will be better equipped to speak wise words when the time is right. As Abraham Lincoln said, "It is better to remain silent and thought a fool than to speak out and remove all doubt."

BACK TO SCHOOL

Take fast hold of instruction;
let her not go: keep her; for she is thy life.
Proverbs 4:13

Life's a classroom chock-full of lessons to be learned. How to walk. How to talk. How to drive a car, poach an egg and make a friend. Some lessons we may learn the hard way, like why it's wise to stay out of debt or why honesty really is the best policy. The best thing we can do once we learn something is to apply it to our lives. That will help us remember it. Because when it comes to painful lessons, we don't want to have to learn them all over again.

A wise student is also an avid pupil of other people's lives. Their successes and failures may teach us what we can't (or don't want to) experience firsthand. Being teachable in this life is one sure way to getting the most, and best, out of it.

THE RIGHT STUFF

The memory of the just is blessed.
Proverbs 10:7

Doing the right thing, the wise thing, the loving thing is the best thing to do in any and every situation. But doing what's ethically, emotionally and spiritually sound is more than a beneficial choice here and now. It's something that pays dividends long into the future.

Every action we take is added to the scrapbook of our memory. Whether that scrapbook will be something we'll look back on with pride, or with regret, depends on the choices we make today. Obviously, the more positive memories we make, the better we'll feel about ourselves and our lives. Do your future self a favor by doing what's best right here and now.

HOW DO I SEE YOU?

Let us not therefore judge one another any more.
Romans 14:13

We all judge others. We may try not to. But it seems we can't help sizing other people up in our heads. We judge whether the scruffy guy holding the sign really needs money or is working a scam. When we make a new friend, we judge whether she's worth our time. Often we judge those who are like us more favorably than those who are not.

If we want to trade in our judgment for love and respect, we need to become aware of what we use as our "sliding scale." Intelligence? Income? Appearance? Whatever it is, it's usually an area of pride in our own lives. The more we allow God to whittle away at our pride, the less judgmental we'll be of those around us.

WISELY WIRED

God is love.
1 John 4:8

Our need for love is hard-wired into us. Without it, we short-circuit. Babies that receive food and shelter, but little love or physical affection, can suffer from what's known as a "failure to thrive." This condition can have long-lasting effects physically, mentally and emotionally.

If we strive to live life on our own, independent of God, we can suffer from a different kind of "failure to thrive." Our longing for acceptance, security, peace, wisdom and confidence are all satisfied through God and His never-ending love. Without Him, we seek them elsewhere, with little success. But when we accept God and His gifts into our lives, we open ourselves up to what our heart's always longed for—the ability to thrive as we become the women we were created to be, one day at a time.

YOU ARE INVITED...

Practice hospitality.
Romans 12:13 NIV

You don't have to be a homemaking maven to invite people over. All you have to be is hospitable. Whether you live in a mansion or a motor home is unimportant. What matters is making your guests feel at home.

Your abode doesn't have to be spotless, your munchies gourmet or your décor anything other than "garage sale" to open your door with a smile. Remember, people are coming to see you, not to judge your grout or your canapés. (If they are, it may be time to edit that guest list!) One thing "happy" people have in common is a circle of supportive friends. Strengthen that circle on your home turf. Watch a movie. Munch chips. Host a potluck. Play a game. Be yourself...and others will feel free to do the same.

A CLEAN SWEEP

A time to search and a time to give up,
a time to keep and a time to throw away.
Ecclesiastes 3:6 NIV

It's hard to feel positive when you're surrounded by chaos. But sometimes, that chaos is of our own making. Your closet is bursting at the seams. Your inbox is overflowing. The kitchen counters are covered with dishes, mail and yesterday's news. Want to make a positive change in your life? Take charge of what's in your control.

Not everyone is born with the organization gene. If clutter feels like your middle name, break down big projects into small ones. Set a timer and work for one hour straight—or even 15 minutes—each day. Even making a little headway in transforming disarray into order will help you feel more comfortable and in control.

JUST DO IT

Be strong and of a good courage;
be not afraid, neither be thou dismayed:
for the LORD thy God is with thee.
Joshua 1:9

You don't have to receive a medal for heroism to be courageous. You can be brave in little ways throughout the day. You can grit your teeth and clean that dead mouse out from under the sink. You can hold your head high when you make a presentation in front of your peers. You can wear a swimsuit over the age of 40.

Anything that gives you pause, yet you tackle anyway, demonstrates courage. It's also a proving ground that can inspire you to take greater risks in the future. Most of the things we fear are not life or death situations. They're simply uncomfortable situations. Risk moving beyond your comfort zone. Show yourself how brave you really are.

HIDE AND SEEK

The LORD God called unto Adam,
and said unto him, Where art thou?
Genesis 3:9

There are three reasons kids hide: they're playing a game, they're scared or they've done something wrong. As adults, we continue to hide from friends and family, God, and ourselves, but it's no game. We're either frightened or ashamed. We may literally pull the blankets over our heads and sleep. Or we may hide in plain sight planted in front of the television, a computer screen or a big bowl of ice cream.

Hiding doesn't change anything. It's just a form of procrastination. If we're honest about wanting to lead a more positive life, we need to come out of hiding. Tackle that unpleasant task. Admit we were wrong. Make a needed change. Then, hold our heads high once more and move on. Why waste another day?

FRIENDLY ADVICE

He that blesseth his friend with a loud voice,
rising early in the morning,
it shall be counted a curse to him.
Proverbs 27:14

Robert Louis Stevenson said, "A friend is a gift you give yourself." And what priceless gifts they are! But the longer we know each other, and the more comfortable we feel around each other, the easier it is to take each other for granted. We begin to expect instead of ask, to overlook instead of appreciate.

The more empathetic we strive to be in our relationships, the less chance there will be that we'll treat our friends with anything less than the love and respect they so richly deserve. By trying to put ourselves physically and emotionally in our friends' shoes, we can better understand what might rub them the wrong way—or make their day.

GOOD GIFTS

Ask, and ye shall receive,
that your joy may be full.
John 16:24

Mothers delight in giving their children good gifts. But that doesn't mean they instantly fulfill every whim and desire kids throw their way. Good moms don't serve their children cake instead of vegetables or hand their toddler a switchblade, no matter how nicely they ask.

God invites you to ask Him for what you need, as well as what you want. He wants you to share with Him the deepest desires of your heart. And like any loving Parent, He wants to bless your life with good things. But God doesn't promise to make certain that all your wishes will come true. He's your heavenly Father, not your fairy tale genie. His deepest desire isn't to make you happy today, but well-equipped to face tomorrow.

LOVE WITHOUT END

God so loved the world,
that he gave his only begotten Son,
that whosoever believeth in him should not perish,
but have everlasting life.
John 3:16

God loves you. He also loves the other 7 billion people on this planet—as well as every individual who'll be born in the future or has lived in the past. Trying to wrap your brain around statements like these can make you feel a bit lost in the crowd!

But God's love is unlike ours. He has an infinite capacity for relationship and communication. (Another fact that's nothing short of mind-boggling...) But just because we can't comprehend how God can love each of us as if there were only one of us doesn't mean He isn't capable of doing it. God is God—and we're not. We may not fathom the depth of His love, but we're infinitely richer for having been on the receiving end of it.

A NOVEL APPROACH

Forget the former things; do not dwell on the past.
See, I am doing a new thing!
Now it springs up; do you not perceive it?
Isaiah 43:18–19 NIV

What's your favorite rut? Maybe it's eating the same thing for breakfast every morning. Taking the same route to work. Buying the same brand of soap. Ruts are comfortable because they're familiar. They demand little risk. But ruts can stunt our growth, particularly when it comes to how we think.

When we view specific situations or people (including ourselves) from a "rut" perspective, we treat today as if it were yesterday. We expect things will remain the same. If someone was mean to us once, we expect that's the way they'll always be. But life isn't static. Situations, and people, change. Don't allow a negative rut to carve itself so deeply into your mind that it becomes a habit. Expect today to hold the unexpected!

STEP-BY-STEP

Let us not become weary in doing good,
for at the proper time we will reap a harvest
if we do not give up.
Galatians 6:9 NIV

Sometimes, life feels like a marathon. We keep plodding forward for what seems like an eternity, but the finish line is still nowhere in sight. How do we keep going when the going gets tough—and shows no sign of letting up?

Perseverance is something we can only learn by doing. But there are a few things that can help us become diligent students. First, keep the finish line in mind. Where do you want to be? Set minor goals along the way. Focus on making it through the next week, the next day, the next hour. Then, take one step. Then, the next. That's all a marathon is, a series of individual steps.

LOST IN TRANSLATION

Keep thy heart with all diligence;
for out of it are the issues of life.
Proverbs 4:23

Our emotions are a gift. Without them, "happiness" would become just an intellectual concept. They enable us to experience the pleasure of joy, love, satisfaction and bliss. They warn us of danger and allow us to empathize with others. But our emotions are not always trustworthy translators of reality. They're swayed by things like past experiences, hormones or stress. They can blow situations way out of proportion and even tell us out-and-out lies.

Just because we feel something is true, or false, doesn't make it so. That's why it's important to let our head join our heart when we make decisions. Ask for advice. Take time to weigh what we know against what we feel. The stronger our emotions are, the more prudent we should be in acting on them.

A BALANCED LIFE

It is vain for you to rise up early, to sit up late,
to eat the bread of sorrows:
for so he giveth his beloved sleep.
Psalm 127:2

In the 1980s, a new word came into use in Japan: kar_shi. A rough translation is "to work oneself to death." Doctors noted that young, otherwise healthy men were dying of strokes or heart attack at a very early age. This was attributed to putting in a 60-plus hour work week in a highly competitive market that demanded excellence.

This may not be your story. But it should at least make you sit up and take note. Work is a gift. A way to support ourselves, develop our skills and contribute to society. But it shouldn't be the focus of your life. Keeping work in a balanced perspective with rest, recreation and relationships, helps you maintain a healthier balance in life.

SOAP (BUBBLE) OPERA

The words of a talebearer are as wounds,
and they go down into the innermost parts.
Proverbs 26:22

Remember those bottles of soap bubbles with the plastic wand inside? Picture yourself blowing those bubbles up, up and away! Once you open your mouth, fill a bubble with air and set it free, you have no control over where it will go. There's also no way to ever get those bubbles back in the bottle once they're released.

The same thing is true when we open our mouths and let gossip fly. We can't control where it goes or unsay what's been said. Gossip is treating someone else's story as our own. If it isn't our own story, sharing it is kind of like plagiarism—wrong on so many levels. Soap bubbles are harmless, but making a soap opera of someone else's struggles is bound to wind up with negative consequences. That's a story best left untold.

MEMBERS OF THE SAME BODY

Whether one member suffer, all the members suffer with it; or one member be honoured, all the members rejoice with it.
1 Corinthians 12:26

The Bible compares God's children to a single, human body. Every part of this special body—every individual—has a unique role to play. Every single part matters. Consider the heart, lungs, feet, eyes... how could we possibly put one above the other in importance?

When we look at other people this way, it helps elevate them in our eyes. We understand that we are one small part of a big picture. What affects one individual, should affect us all. That means the good we do is not just "good" for us, but good for everyone we're connected to. We have the power to lift the body up, or bring it down. Which will we choose today?

TURN THE PAGE

Be admonished:
of making many books there is no end.
Ecclesiastes 12:12

Even way back when the book of Ecclesiastes was written, about 3,000 years ago, books abounded. People had plenty of ideas to share, arguments to make and creativity to put on display. With the invention of the printing press, and then e-books, imagine how the number of volumes have multiplied! It's estimated that roughly 130 million titles are available worldwide today.

Obviously, you don't have time to read them all. So, choose wisely. Read the books and magazines that celebrate what's good and of lasting value. Whether you're learning something new, or simply being entertained, remember that what you mull over in your mind affects your mood and perspective. Read what encourages you, instead of what leads you to feel cynical or down in the dumps.

BOTTOM LINE

A generous person will prosper;
whoever refreshes others will be refreshed.
Proverbs 11:25 NIV

When you hear the word "miser" what picture comes to mind? Chances are it's of a stringy-haired, tight-lipped old man with a furrowed brow, clutching his purse-strings as if his life depended on it. But an attractive modern-day woman can be just as accurate a portrait—if she refuses to hold what she owns with open hands.

Our ability to make money is a gift. Not everyone receives that gift in equal measure. The money we make is a tool to be used, not a treasure to be put on display. One way of putting it to use is to benefit others. Sharing our wealth is just another way of sharing our love.

TO THINE OWN SELF BE KIND

The mountains shall depart, and the hills be removed; but my kindness shall not depart from thee.
Isaiah 54:10

Be kind to yourself. Linger over your latte. Sing your heart out behind the steering wheel. Snuggle under the blankets a little longer on a Saturday morning. Wear the red sweater, just because it makes you feel pretty. Focus on loving others, instead of that unwanted five pounds. Relish the little things. Forgive yourself. Laugh at your mistakes... then try again.

Life is not one big self-improvement session. God created us to celebrate, as well as to serve. If God's kindness to us is never-ending, certainly He wants us to treat ourselves in kind. Literally. This isn't a license to become self-centered. It's merely an invitation to enjoy what God's so graciously given.

A HEALTHY ATTITUDE

I pray that you may enjoy good health
and that all may go well with you,
even as your soul is getting along well.
3 John 1:2 NIV

Today, it isn't considered pop science to acknowledge a mind/body connection. How we think can affect how we feel. That means that those with a positive view of life, as opposed to those who view the glass of life as half-empty, will feel better physically—even when they're sick!

Your spirit, as well as your mind, is tied into your well-being. When you're leaning on God, instead of trying to run the world all by yourself, you're obviously going to feel less stressed. That takes less of a toll physically on your body. So, do yourself a favor. Rest in God's peace, rely on His strength and trust in His plans. Your body will thank you for it.

BATTLE CRY

Some trust in chariots, and some in horses:
but we will remember the name of the LORD our God.
Psalm 20:7

We can acknowledge there are battles to fight in this life and still maintain a positive outlook. Being a half-full kind of woman doesn't mean overlooking what may threaten to drain your glass. It simply means we keep things in the proper perspective. We remember that any battle we face, we never fight alone.

When warriors fight literal battles, they do what they can to protect themselves. At one time, warriors used swords and shields while fighting in chariots or on horseback. Times have changed. Our methods of protection, and defense, have advanced. But we haven't come so far that we need God's help less than those who lived in not-so-modern times. God's still near. And we still need Him.

SIGNED WITH PRIDE

A good name is rather to be chosen than great riches, and loving favour rather than silver and gold.
Proverbs 22:1

When you think of great artists, what names come to mind? DaVinci? Picasso? Van Gogh? If you found a $5 painting at a garage sale with one of those names at the bottom of the canvas, chances are you'd snatch it up lickety-split. Those names are a sign of artistic genius. That makes their work valuable and desirable.

In a way, you sign your name to everything you say and do. You may create more works of "heart," than works of art, but each one is a portrait of your character. Take pride in signing your name to it today. Earn your own self-respect. Do the best you can with what you have. In your own unique way, paint today with strokes of genius.

PUTTING LIFE IN FOCUS

Blessed are the pure in heart:
for they shall see God.
Matthew 5:8

What we look for, we usually find. If we're looking for proof that life is fundamentally disappointing, we'll find it. If we're looking for things to celebrate in a seemingly ordinary day, we'll find them. And if we're sincerely looking for God, we'll see evidence of His fingerprints all over our lives.

When we're looking for an invisible God, the ways we see Him will differ from how we see the eye chart at the optometrist's office. Improbable coincidences, unparalleled beauty, unexpected joy, unexplainable peace, whispers of wisdom and truth... these are glimpses of God. As we keep our eyes, heart and mind open for signs of Him, we'll inevitably observe what's good and admirable along the way. A God-focused life can't help but be a positive one.

THE BLESSING OF A THANKFUL HEART

I have learned the secret of being content in any and every situation, whether well fed or hungry, whether living in plenty or in want.
Philippians 4:12 NIV

How can we feel happy and content one minute, then resentful and dissatisfied the next? Because we have very short memories. Whatever is happening right now has a much bigger hold on us emotionally than what happened last week...or even ten minutes ago. If only we could remember all the reasons we're feeling grateful today when tomorrow rolls around.

Creating touchstones can help. For instance, when you're grateful for something, write it down in a journal or on a piece of paper that you place in a jar. When you're feeling down, read what you've written. It's hard to feel discontent when you're focused on how much you have to be grateful for.

LIFE ISN'T A SITCOM

The heart of the righteous studieth to answer.
Proverbs 15:28

If TV were an actual window onto real life, you'd think sarcasm was the most common form of communication. Luckily, television presents more of a caricature that exaggerates reality instead of reality itself. But television does more than entertain. It also informs and educates—in it's own off-beat way. And we tend to imitate what we see.

Quick-witted sarcastic retorts are highly regarded on the tube. But when speaking to real people in real life, they don't aid honest communication. They hinder it. They may showcase your intellectual prowess and sense of humor, but they also display a lack of love and respect for those you're speaking with. Weigh your words. Answer wisely, instead of with a wise-crack. It's more important to build relationships, than an audience.

CONUNDRUM

Be not forgetful to entertain strangers:
for thereby some have entertained angels unawares.
Hebrews 13:2

The Bible tells us there's a spiritual world that exists beyond the realm of our senses. But sometimes, that world overlaps our own. When we hear about unexplained mysteries, miracles and encounters, we raise our eyebrows in wonder. We may doubt the validity of these claims—until something truly out of the ordinary happens to us.

Leaving room for God to work outside the box of our senses and sensibilities may feel a bit uncomfortable. We like to explain away what's out of our control. But a finite brain cannot comprehend an infinite God. Acknowledging the possibility there's more to life than can be fully explained is a glass half-full way of relating to the world—both the physical and the spiritual.

WHAT'S YOUR MOTIVATION?

Surely goodness and mercy shall follow me
all the days of my life:
and I will dwell in the house of the LORD for ever.
Psalm 23:6

Do we really "dwell" with God or just drop in for a visit when we've exhausted our own resources? If the truth be told, most of us would rather keep Him at arm's length, using God as our "life line" instead of trusting Him as a loving Father.

That's because we don't fully trust His plans for us. If we let Him in too close, we're afraid he'll ship us off to the jungle as a missionary or force us to give away all we own to the poor. It's true that we don't know the extent of His plans for us. But if we consider His goodness and mercy, we'll more likely be drawn to His character, and less likely to question His motives. Those motives are always rooted in love.

THE MAIN ATTRACTION

As a jewel of gold in a swine's snout,
so is a fair woman which is without discretion.
Proverbs 11:22

We all want to be attractive in the physical sense. Chances are you take a shower, shave your legs, put on a bit of make-up and wear clothes that fit. But an "attractive" woman literally means being a woman who draws others to herself. She has a magnetic personality—with a positive charge.

It takes more than appearances to appeal to others. It takes strength of character. When others feel accepted and welcomed by someone who feels good about herself, they're more likely to hang around and get to know her better. Selfish traits such as boasting, rudeness and insensitivity repel. Other-focused traits such as humility, compassion and love attract. How attractive are you today?

LET'S PULL TOGETHER

I saw that all toil and all achievement spring
from one person's envy of another.
This too is meaningless, a chasing after the wind.
Ecclesiastes 4:4 NIV

There are two ways of looking at other people: as community or as competition. If we choose the latter, the way we view ourselves changes along with the way we view others. We'll live in a state of constant comparison, trying to prove our worth, while we judge others with a critical, and often envious, eye.

A more positive perspective—God's perspective—is to be drawn together as a community. When we focus on celebrating each other's individual gifts, experiences and personalities we cooperate and appreciate, instead of envy and compare. We're each a uniquely created masterpiece. By pulling together, we make a beautifully diverse global gallery.

OF MOUNTAINS AND MOLEHILLS

Know therefore this day,
and consider it in thine heart.
Deuteronomy 4:39

Which is bigger, a marble or a mountain? You're thinking, "Is this a trick question?" Yet if you look off toward a distant mountain while holding a marble right in front of your eye, the marble seems pretty mammoth. It's so "big" it can block out the mountain entirely.

It's all about perspective. Things appear larger depending how close they are to us. That's why "little things" so easily masquerade as "big things" in our lives. They're in our face! A flat tire, a careless comment, the cancellation of a highly-anticipated event...these don't signal the end of the world. But it can feel like it. Step back and take a fresh look. Don't allow a marble to take a mountain's worth of time, energy or emotion from your day.

LET IT GO

Forgive as the Lord forgave you.
Colossians 3:13 NIV

A grudge is a dangerous pet. You have to feed it to keep it—and what it's hungry for is bitterness, anger, resentment and pride. But what it's secretly doing while you're feeding it is eating you. Stress, anxiety, a loss of mental focus and even depression are all potential by-products of withholding forgiveness from someone who's hurt you.

Do yourself a favor and set that grudge free. Forgiveness is not forgetting or minimizing what someone's done. It's extending grace, undeserved and unconditional. It's handing that list of grievances you've been holding onto over to God. Let Him handle what's just. As for you, choose to live life grudge-free. You might be surprised to discover the freedom you feel most is your own.

YOU CAN'T SET THEM IN STONE

Boast not thyself of to morrow;
for thou knowest not what a day may bring forth.
Proverbs 27:1

It's important to make plans. It enables us to set goals and make the most of our time. But plans are made up of individual puzzle pieces. Every so often one of them goes AWOL. When that happens we need to accept that the final picture will look different from the one we'd expected to see.

The more flexible we are, the more easily we can bend our expectations without breaking down. Certainly, we're bound to feel disappointed when things go awry. But disappointment doesn't have to be synonymous with disaster. A change in direction can spark unexpected creativity. It can lead to an opportunity we may have missed if we hadn't been detoured. So, go ahead and plan. Just leave room for the unexpected.

STOP, LOOK AND LISTEN

Consider the lilies of the field, how they grow...
Matthew 6:28

Little things can teach us a lot, if we make an effort to slow down and pay attention to what they have to say. Consider a simple wildflower. God provides everything it needs to grow. He adorns it with all the beauty of an artistic masterpiece—even though there's a good chance that not one single person will ever bend down and take notice of it. But if we do, the sight of a tiny bud, pushing up through the concrete of a busy sidewalk so it can drink in the sunlight and bloom, encourages us to persevere, despite all odds.

God's infused life lessons, messages of encouragement and little jolts of joy in everything from the stars above us to the tiniest of flowers below. It pays to pay attention to the small things.

A BACKWARD GLANCE

Remember the days of old,
consider the years of many generations.
Deuteronomy 32:7

At times, taking a look at what's behind us can give us the strength we need to move forward. It can encourage and enlighten us. It can reassure us we're headed in the right direction. It can help us appreciate how much we've grown.

Keeping a journal is an effective way to keep the past close-at-hand without dwelling on it. It doesn't have to be a time-consuming project. Jot down your goals. Write out your prayers. Capture the essence of today's highs and lows in just a sentence or two. On occasion, reassess the road you've traveled. Celebrate how far you've come. Perhaps you've achieved a long-desired goal or broken a negative pattern that's been passed down through the generations. Commend yourself for a job well done! Then, continue moving forward.

A POSITIVE REFLECTION

A virtuous woman is a crown to her husband.
Proverbs 12:4

Not every woman is married, but for those of us who are, we have the opportunity to honor our husband by living a life that reflects positively on him. When our kindness, compassion, wisdom, diligence and humility shine through in what we say and do, it reflects well on our spouse, as well as on ourselves. Our loving, positive actions and attitudes will make him feel good and look good. After all, he's the one that such a "virtuous" woman has chosen to spend her life with!

It would be wonderful if your spouse's exemplary life reflected as well on you as yours does on him. But this isn't a 50/50 deal, where you'll make him proud if he does the same for you. True virtue does what's right, just because it's right—without expecting anything in return.

A WELL-TRAVELED WOMAN

The earth is the LORD'S, and the fulness thereof; the world, and they that dwell therein.
Psalm 24:1

To have a broad, global perspective on life, we need to know a little about the world, as well as the people who dwell on it. Not all of us have the time, or financial ability, to circumnavigate the globe. But that doesn't mean we can't become world explorers. We can read books, watch movies and talk to people who've lived or traveled to places we might not even be able to locate on a map.

The better grasp we have of how diverse the world and its people are, the more we'll broaden our minds—and our hearts. Encountering cultural, spiritual or individual diversity stretches our personal boundaries and preconceived notions. It reminds us that we are one small part of one very big picture.

QUICK FIX

God is our refuge and strength,
a very present help in trouble.
Psalm 46:1

If you're feeling pessimistic, chances are an "if only" has taken up residence in your heart. "If only I had a job..." "...a child." "...her life instead of mine." Whatever your own personal "if only," it's tempting to believe that everything would be okay "if only" God would answer this one prayer.

But we're complex creatures. We can't be as easily fixed as a toy that's lost a wheel. The inner and outer workings of our lives are infinitely complex. Our "if onlys" are intricately related to other, deeper, issues. What's your "if only" really about? Insecurity? Fear? Loneliness? Invite God to help you get to the root of the real problem. He doesn't promise an easy fix. But He's your best hope for a permanent one.

THE SIMPLE LIFE

Understanding is a wellspring of life unto him that hath it.
Proverbs 16:22

Over 150 years ago, Henry David Thoreau wrote, "Our life is frittered away by detail...Simplify, simplify!" Consider how much more complex our lives are now than they were then. Trying to keep so many plates in the air (or passwords in our heads) can drive us to distraction. And every day that drive seems to get shorter!

But there are things we can do to simplify our lives. Little things... Read the paper or watch the evening news. Work one positive habit into your daily routine (like starting a new exercise program) for 30 days before starting another. Be satisfied with a less extensive wardrobe. Choose a quick and easy hairstyle. What can you do today that will help you not fritter your life away?

THE NOT-SO-HUMBLE MUMBLE

Whoso keepeth his mouth and his tongue keepeth his soul from troubles.
Proverbs 21:23

A word muttered under your breath. A roll of your eyes. A heavy sigh. You can complain without out-and-out grumbling. But even if you keep from announcing your criticism or displeasure to those around you, your mind gets the message loud and clear. And it repeats it ad nauseum.

Inner grumblings can be as destructive as full-on rants. Sure, you're not dragging anyone else down with you. But you're focusing on the negative and wallowing in it, instead of dealing with it. Check your own attitude. Does it need an adjustment? Or is there a real problem you need to address? Perhaps there's a commitment you need to reexamine or a relationship that could use a little honest intervention. Deal with the grumble while it's still just a mumble.

DOLLARS AND SENSE

The rich and poor meet together:
the LORD is the maker of them all.
Proverbs 22:2

Some call it destiny. Others call it dumb luck. But the truth is, a large part of our life story is determined by the hand of God. Where we're born. Who our parents are. How fast our metabolism is. Whether we're tone deaf or have perfect pitch. Even our financial situation is heavily influenced by factors such as our nationality, our parents' economic and educational situation, our health and our IQ. We can pull ourselves up by our own bootstraps, but those straps only reach so far.

It isn't how much we've been given that's important. It's how we use what we have. Money isn't the bottom line. It's how well we love God and others. That's where happiness, contentment and a positive outlook are ultimately found.

SPEAK UP

My mouth shall speak truth.
Proverbs 8:7

It's easier to remain silent than speak up, particularly if you know those around you may not be in agreement with what you have to say. But the easy thing isn't always the right thing. There are times when the voice of reason needs to be heard loud and clear. And sometimes that "voice" happens to be yours.

One person can make a difference. Consider Martin Luther, or his namesake Martin Luther King, Jr.. Change—whether it's inspiring social change or an individual to change his or her opinion—begins with a thought followed by a word. You may have the perfect perspective that helps someone else see what's right and true. Your opinion and experience matter. So do your words. So, let them be heard!

BATTLE SCARS

I have fought a good fight,
I have finished my course, I have kept the faith.
2 Timothy 4:7

Are you ashamed of a scar you bear? It could be a physical scar from a burn, a battle with cancer or an accident. Or perhaps it's an emotional scar left by a broken relationship, difficult childhood or traumatic event.

Don't hide your scar. It isn't a deformity. It's more like a medal for bravery and valor, a sign that you fought a hard battle and survived. The more open you are about your scars, the more you'll encourage those around you to be open with the tough things they've faced in their lives. Honesty, authenticity and transparency are keys to sharing the heart of who we are with others and inviting them to do the same.

BIG PICTURE PERSPECTIVE

Set your minds on things above,
not on earthly things.
Colossians 3:2 NIV

Some people believe they're looking at life from a positive perspective, when they're really living in denial. Ignoring conflict, holding back your tears, making light of what's breaking your heart or burying your pain in busyness may look like you're living a glass half-full kind of life. But it's really refusing to deal with reality.

Instead of donning rose-colored glasses, put on God-centered ones. This isn't accomplished by trying harder to think more positively. It requires a full-blown heart transplant. When we choose to follow God, our hearts—and therefore our lives—begin to change. So does our perspective. We begin to see things in light of eternity, instead of just this transient minute. By re-focusing on God's big picture, we can be more positive about our past, our present and our future.

MIRROR, MIRROR...IN MY HEART

Your beauty should not come from outward adornment...
Rather, it should be that of your inner self,
the unfading beauty of a gentle and quiet spirit.
1 Peter 3:3–4 NIV

Once upon a time, there was a certain fairy tale princess who convinced future generations of women that finding the right shoe really could change their lives. But the prince, the fairy godmother, the magic slipper...they're all make-believe. Yet some of us act as though the perfect shoe, or outfit, actually is the secret to living happily ever after.

There's nothing wrong with heading to the mall now and then. But if what you're really shopping for is a new "you," you're going to be disappointed once the novelty of your purchase wears off. You can't buy your way into becoming someone else. Only by becoming comfortable with who you really are will you feel beautiful, regardless of your attire.

HOME SWEET HOME

In the midst of the church will I sing praise unto thee.
Hebrews 2:12

You may not see yourself as a "church" person. You may think believing in God is one thing, but going to church every Sunday is quite another. But becoming part of a church family can be a steadfast source of encouragement. Not only can you learn more about God, but more about unconditional love—firsthand.

A church is simply a group of people who wrestle together with questions of faith while upholding one another in friendship and prayer. Everyone is imperfect. Just like you. Over time, you'll discover you have more in common than you may think. You'll also gain accountability, stability, community and an opportunity to serve and be served. Look for a church that makes you feel at home. There's a family out there waiting for you!

SPRING THAW

Thou hast made summer and winter.
Psalm 74:17

When the ground is covered with snow and the trees are barren, stripped of their fruit and leaves, it can appear that what was once green and growing is now lifeless...and useless. But below the surface, roots are still growing, sap is still running and life continues on.

The same is true during certain seasons of our lives. Our days may appear to be just, plain barren. Joy seems like a distant memory. We feel we're not making any headway. God remains silent. We begin to doubt if things can actually change for the better. But like the hidden growth of winter, things are changing slowly. They're just invisible to our eyes. Hold onto the promise of spring. It's burgeoning just below the surface.

YOUR ARTISTIC BENT

Be ye glad and rejoice for ever in that which I create.
Isaiah 65:18

You were created, well...to create! It's a trait that's passed down from your heavenly Father to you. You don't have to become a professional artist, bestselling author or celebrated chef to let those creative juices flow. Just take time to do what you love.

Take photographs. Make quilts. Sing in the car. Even playing sports, hiking, bowling, bird-watching—or any of your favorite hobbies—can be classified as a creative act. Why do you think they are called recreation? You are re-creating something new by challenging your brain to learn and grow in novel directions. Don't think of recreation as "wasting time." It's time well-spent in creating a new, more creative you.

HERE KITTY, KITTY, KITTY...

I have made the earth,
the man and the beast that are upon the ground.
Jeremiah 27:5

If you want to boost your immune system and lower your stress, take a trip to an animal shelter. But don't come home empty-handed. Caring for a pet has a lot of positive benefits. Children who grow up around animals have lower rates of asthma and all-around sick days. A pet's antics can also elicit smiles when you need them most.

But when choosing a pet, choose one that fits your lifestyle—and is pet-able. The act of petting a dog or cat (or a ferret, for that matter) can lower your blood pressure and relieve muscle tension. Pouring your love into a furry friend is also a great way to express your emotions in a physical way at the end of a long day.

"NO" PROBLEM

Let your speech be always with grace,
seasoned with salt,
that ye may know how ye ought to answer every man.
Colossians 4:6

Not every question can be answered with "yes" or "no." But too often we waffle on ones that do. For some of us, it's easier to just say "yes" than to deal with the repercussions of saying "no."

It's true we want to stretch ourselves. We shouldn't only commit to things that are fun, easy or require no sacrifice on our part. But if the opinions of others, or the feeling that if we don't do things they won't be done right, is causing us to become "yes women," it's time we changed our ways—and our answer. "No" is a complete sentence. We don't have to explain our "why." We can politely decline and save our "yes" for another day.

AT A LOSS

To every thing there is a season,
and a time to every purpose under the heaven:
A time to be born, and a time to die.
Ecclesiastes 3:1–2

Grief is one of the heaviest burdens we'll ever carry. Losing someone we love isn't a problem that can be fixed. It's a wound that never fully heals. When it's fresh, it's hard to believe it will ever heal at all. To compound our sorrow, grief is often accompanied by anger with God or a belief that He's abandoned us—either He doesn't see or doesn't care.

When you're buried beneath grief, don't run from God. Go ahead and rant at Him. He can take it. Then, run toward Him. His love for you, and the one you've lost, is solid ground in the shifting sands of emotion. His assurance of heaven is a comforting balm. Moment-by-moment, He'll help you find a new way to continue living and loving.

BABY YOURSELF

My times are in thy hand.
Psalm 31:15

Babies are pretty straight-forward. They sleep when they're tired. They eat when they're hungry. They cry when they're in pain and laugh when they're amused. To a point, their own natural rhythms dictate the schedule of their day.

As adults, we often work against our natural rhythms. We sign up for the night shift. We eat not because we're hungry, but because we're bored. We stay up late to watch the end of a movie, even though we've slept through half of it. By accommodating our natural rhythms into our daily schedules as much as possible, we'll be more productive. We'll also feel more at ease. For instance, if you're most productive in the mornings, tackle your toughest tasks then. Listen to your body. It has something important to say.

FAIL SWITCH

Thou wilt keep him in perfect peace,
whose mind is stayed on thee:
because he trusteth in thee.
Isaiah 26:3–4

Stress isn't all bad. It actually has a positive purpose. But it can cause memory loss, hypertension, depression, stomach upsets and even fertility issues. But that's only when we forget to turn our stress button into the "off" position. Unfortunately, the longer we allow stress to take its toll, the harder it is to turn off.

To shut stress down, we need to go back to where it began—in our brain. How we perceive a situation is what sends our brain, and then our body, into overdrive. When our thinking is in line with God's big picture, we have an option beside "fight" or "flight." We have access to a button marked "trust." It's a fail switch that replaces stress with peace and perspective.

SIZING YOURSELF UP

In the morning will I direct my prayer unto thee,
and will look up.
Psalm 5:3

Every morning we do the same thing—get dressed. What we choose to wear says a lot about how we see ourselves. Forget about style for a moment and ask yourself this one question: Am I wearing the size that fits?

Wearing oversized clothes is often a sign that you're trying to hide yourself and your perceived flaws. If you're squeezing into clothes that are too small, you may be trying to look younger, thinner or are simply refusing to accept that your maturing body has graduated into a larger size. It's hard to feel positive about life if you don't feel positive about yourself. Go ahead. Work to get in shape. Meanwhile, don't overlook the benefits of accepting, and dressing for, where you are right now.

THE KEY TO LOVING WELL

Delight thyself also in the LORD:
and he shall give thee the desires of thine heart.
Psalm 37:4

The heart of every individual is like a combination lock; it takes a unique set of moves to open it. Only when our hearts are open can we give and receive love fully. Our desires try to convince us that they hold the proper combination. But our desires are not the most intuitive, or accurate, of locksmiths. They point to what feels good, looks good or what today's culture tells us is a good way to fill our deepest longings.

God created our hearts, so He's the best judge when it comes to their care. He knows what will open them—and what desires will lead us in directions where this can take place. The more our desires resemble God's own, the more positive paths we'll find ourselves on.

HOLD ONTO HOPE

With God, all things are possible.
Matthew 19:26

At one time, people believed it was impossible for someone to walk on the moon, travel faster than the speed of sound or sail around the world without falling off the edge. Today things that were once thought impossible happen every day.

Is there anything in your life that you've resigned to the "impossible" list? Getting out of debt? Reconciling a relationship? Reaching your goal weight? Breaking a lifelong habit? If over time, mere mortals can make what's seemingly impossible happen, imagine how much greater the odds are when God is involved? Don't lose hope. Hand your "impossible" list over to God. He'll either turn it into reality or transform it into something wholly different—turning your desires or your direction toward a wiser path.

ABOVE AND BEYOND

I have not stopped giving thanks for you, remembering you in my prayers.
Ephesians 1:16 NIV

It's good to give thanks to God for all He's done. But why stop there? There are people in our lives who've also helped us along the way. They've shown us unexpected kindness, generosity or support. They've gone above and beyond just doing us a favor or lending a hand. They've loved us...sometimes when we least deserved it.

If faces come to mind right now of people who've been this kind of friend to you, tell them. Give them a call. Write them a letter. Send a bouquet of flowers. Let them know the difference they've made in your life. Your words of thanks can make a positive difference in theirs.

BLESSED BEAUTY ROUTINE

Bless the LORD, O my soul,
and forget not all his benefits.
Psalm 103:2

It's what goes on behind the scenes that help us look our best. A 10-minute walk around the block. A good night's sleep. Maintaining healthy, balanced relationships. Taking time to laugh. Focusing on the positive. Nurturing a thankful heart. Transforming each worry into a prayer... Practices like these are good for our bodies, as well as our souls. That's because when we feel good, it shows.

Spending less time looking in the mirror and more time reflecting on how we can care for what matters most in our lives is a beauty routine that never grows old. It allows the beauty that's inside to make its way to the outside in wonderful ways.

DREAMS WORTH CHASING

Thou openest thine hand,
and satisfiest the desire of every living thing.
Psalm 145:16

We all have a secret ambition. Perhaps you want to see the Eiffel Tower. Or maybe you want to write a novel, learn to fly fish or hike Mount Kilimanjaro. Whatever your secret ambition, it does your heart good to move beyond the stage of simply dreaming about it. Your fondest dreams are an integral part of who you are.

Ask God for insight into what to do with your secret longings. Some are worth pursuing. Some may be "counterfeit," like dreaming of becoming a pop star when what you really want is to feel worthy of admiration—including your own. Allow God to help you sort and plan. Then, follow-through and pursue ones worth becoming reality.

A FRIENDLY INVITATION

This is my beloved, and this is my friend.
Song of Solomon 5:16

A circle is a wonderful geometric form. You can expand it without breaking it apart. The same is true with a circle of friends. There's always room to add one more. But when life gets busy, or we get comfortable, it's easy to become complacent. We declare our dance card full. We don't feel we have enough time or energy to love more people.

But not every acquaintance has to be our BFF. If we stop reaching out, we may miss out on a bona-fide friend for life. We may also wind up surrounding ourselves with people who are similar in personality, interests and points of view. We need friends who stretch us and challenge us to grow. One way to do that is to continually expand our circle of friends slowly, and thoughtfully, over time.

BREATHING ROOM

Every day will I bless thee.
Psalm 145:2

It's wise to build a little extra margin into our schedule. Because we know it's gonna happen... traffic, a flat tire, a sick child, a forgotten lunch, misplaced keys. Or maybe we're going to need to do something twice, like make a second piece of toast after the first one is, well...toast.

If we try to keep our schedule less than 75% full, we allow room for error and inconvenience without pushing ourselves, and our stress levels, into overdrive. Leave more space between appointments. Schedule in a slot for the "unknown" each afternoon where you can catch up on anything that takes longer than anticipated. When the unexpected happens, if we've already made allowances for it, we'll be more likely to still view it as a "good" day.

TOGETHER IS BETTER

We are labourers together with God.
1 Corinthians 3:9

"Do it myself!" is a popular declaration among toddlers. Yet plenty of grown women continue to act them out every day. We don't ask for help and are reluctant to accept it when offered. Maybe we feel we get more accomplished, more expediently, on our own. Perhaps we're afraid others won't do things "our way." Maybe they'll let us down—or show us up!

It's true that when we delegate, things don't always turn out the way we'd planned. Sometimes, they turn out even better. We need the energy, creativity and community that working together brings. Not to mention how good it is for our humility. So, whether it's at our workplace or at home, let's share the load. Working together makes it so much easier to carry.

TIE UP LOOSE ENDS

Whatsoever ye do, do it heartily,
as to the Lord.
Colossians 3:23

Little things can weigh as heavily on your mind as big things. They are an underlying stress that you can easily get rid of—if you just took the time to cross them off your list. So, why not make the time?

Schedule a "Someday" every couple of months. Use it to do all of the things you've planned on getting to "some day." Replace the batteries in your smoke detectors. Hem those pants. Change the oil in your car. Sew on that button. Toss the expired things in your fridge. Write that thank you note. Tie up whatever loose ends that have lately been tying your thoughts in knots. Make a list of the little things, then cross things off one-by-one. You'll feel ten pounds lighter by the end of the day.

PROMISES, PROMISES...

God is faithful.
1 Corinthians 1:9

A familiar saying asserts that "promises are made to be broken." In essence, what it's saying is "you can't trust people to be faithful." Do you think that's true? Is it true about you? When you say you'll be somewhere or do something, do you follow through unless some unforeseen disaster strikes?

Strong relationships rest on a solid foundation of trust. If you make a promise and then break it, perhaps it never was a true promise in the first place. It may have been more of a "perhaps..." or an "if it's convenient" or an "if something better doesn't come along." You're as good as your word. Literally. Make promises thoughtfully. Then, fulfill them faithfully.

WHAT DOES TOMORROW HOLD?

"I know the plans I have for you," declares the LORD,
"plans to prosper you and not to harm you,
plans to give you hope and a future."
Jeremiah 29:11 NIV

Where are you headed from here? God knows. Your future may lead you precisely in the direction you expect or it could take you somewhere you couldn't have pictured in your wildest dreams. Whatever your future holds, hope and purpose will be an integral part of it. God doesn't send His kids out on a wild goose chase.

So look toward tomorrow with eagerness and expectancy. The next chapter in your story is about to be written. God supplies the outline, but the decisions you make and the perspective you hold, will influence how your story will unfold. Make it a classic, filled with love, beauty and the very best you have to give.

The LORD bless you and keep you;
the LORD make his face shine
on you and be gracious to you;
the LORD turn his face toward
you and give you peace.

Numbers 6:24–26 NIV